South West Coast Path
North Cornwall Coast

Bude to Land's End

GW00778056

Part of the England Coast Path

Text: *Dennis and Jan Kelsall*
Series editor: *Tony Bowerman*
Photographs: *Dennis and Jan Kelsall, Tony Bowerman, Wikipedia Commons/John Maynard Friedman, Adobe Stock, Alamy, Dreamstime, Shutterstock*

Design: *Carl Rogers and Laura Hodgkinson*

© *Northern Eye Books Limited 2019*

Dennis and Jan Kelsall have asserted their rights under the Copyright, Designs and Patents Act, 1988 to be identified as the author of this work. All rights reserved.

This book contains mapping data licensed from the Ordnance Survey with the permission of the Controller of Her Majesty's Stationery Office.
© *Crown copyright 2019. All rights reserved. License number 100047867*

Northern Eye Books
ISBN 978-1-908632-72-2

A CIP catalogue record for this book is available from the British Library.

www.northerneyebooks.co.uk

Cover: *Wheal Coates Engine House (Walk 7)*

Important Advice: The routes described in this book are undertaken at the reader's own risk. Walkers should take into account their level of fitness, wear suitable footwear and clothing, and carry food and water. It is also advisable to take the relevant Ordnance Survey map with you in case you get lost and leave the area covered by our maps.

Whilst every care has been taken to ensure the accuracy of the route directions, the publishers cannot accept responsibility for errors or omissions, or for changes in the details given. Nor can the publisher and copyright owners accept responsibility for any consequences arising from the use of this book.

If you find any inaccuracies in either the text or maps, please write or email us at the address below. Thank you.

First published in 2019 by:

Northern Eye Books Limited
Northern Eye Books, Tattenhall, Cheshire CH3 9PX

tony@northerneyebooks.com
www.northerneyebooks.co.uk

@northerneyebooks
@northerneyeboo

For sales enquiries, please call 01928 723 744

www.englandcoastpath.co.uk
www.northerneyebooks.co.uk

Contents

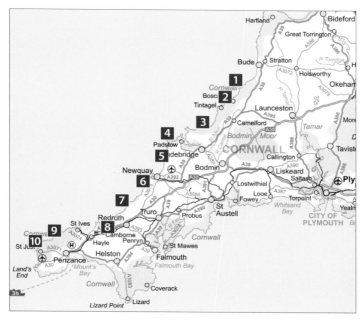

South West Coast Path

Running for 630 miles from Minehead in Somerset, around the tip of Land's End and back to South Haven Point at the mouth of Poole Harbour in Dorset, the South West Coast Path is Britain's longest National Trail. Bordered by the Bristol and English channels and looking out to the open Atlantic, it encompasses some of England's most spectacular and wildest coastline, where the diversity of plant, animal and insect life can be stunning. The seas, coves and surrounding hinterland has been a dramatic setting for a gloriously rich history, which have inspired countless tales of romance, drama and intrigue.

This series of Top Ten Walks explores highlights along the way; showcasing its natural beauty, wildlife and heritage and provoking imagination. Who knows, you may be inspired to come back to tackle the complete trail.

St Ives is a popular seaside town famous for its many artists and galleries

North Cornwall Coast

From Bude to the western-most tip of England at Land's End, Cornwall's northern coast has a character all its own. Much of its 140 miles is set against the open Atlantic, whose winter storms and thundering waves have sculpted a rugged coastline of formidable cliffs. Tiny, wave-washed coves and zawns contrast with expansive beaches and dunes, the wild scenery often spilling offshore to half submerged reefs, stacks and islands. Habitation and farming generally stand back to leave an untouched coast, although in places the relics of 19th-century mining remain as intriguing monuments to an industry that spanned 4,000 years. The holiday resorts of St Ives and Newquay attract summer crowds, but elsewhere, the coast is often deserted, with only seabirds for company.

"Welcome to Cornwall.
Twinned with Heaven"

Devon-Cornwall border road sign

TOP 10 **Walks:** North Cornwall's Coast

FROM CORNWALL'S HIGHEST CLIFFS TO REMOTE, TIDE-WASHED COVES, these walks explore the finest sections of North Cornwall's coast. Admire attractive fishing villages such as Port Quin and Port Isaac, or explore geology, from shifting dunes at Holywell to ancient ore-bearing granites of the far south west. The rich mining heritage is vividly revealed between Cape Cornwall and Levant, with impressive remains around St Agnes too. Bedruthan's profusion of stacks is not to be missed, while inland highlights include the viewpoint of St Agnes Beacon and Trehidy Country Park's woods. Wildflowers and birds abound and almost every walk offers an opportunity to dip your toe in the sea.

Crackington Haven — page 8

Port Quin & Port Isaac — page 14

Pentire Point — page 20

Trevose Head — page 26

On the South West Coast Path looking towards Cambeak headland

Crackington Haven

By a stream through a secluded wooded valley to Cornwall's highest cliff

What to expect:
Exposed coast and some steep paths

Distance/Time: 8 kilometres/ 5 miles. Allow 3 to 3½ hours

Start: Crackington Haven car park (pay and display)

Grid ref: SX 143 967

Ordnance Survey map: Explorer 111: Bude, Boscastle & Tintagel

Refreshment: The Combe Barton Inn | 01840 230345 | www.thecombebartoninn OR The Cabin Café | 01840 230238 | www.cabincafecrackington.co.uk

Walk Outline

From the village, the route heads through the wooded Ludon valley before scaling its steep, grassy slopes to Trevigue. Crossing the lane to meet the Coast Path, there is then a strenuous there-and-back climb onto High Cliff, the loftiest spot along Cornwall's coast. The return follows the coast above The Strangles and Little Strand to Cambeak, eventually dropping steeply to Tremoutha and undulating back to Crackington Haven

Rock pool explorer

Crackington Haven

Despite boats having to beach on the sand for loading and unloading at low tide, Crackington Haven developed as a small port, with coal and limestone being landed in exchange for slate and farm produce. The quarries were profitable and the early 19th century saw ambitious plans to build a breakwater and deep-water harbour plus a rail link to Launceston. However, all came to naught; the industry declined and the quarry manager's house became a pub, while the railway stopped at Otterham, five miles away. But perhaps it was all a blessing for the village has retained its character and fine beach.

Bluebells

The Walk

1. Out of the **car park**, turn left up the hill. Keep left with the main lane at a fork, but then take the next turning off on the right. Walk up past **houses** to the very end of the drive.

2. A footpath continues ahead between outgrown hedges, leading to a **bridge** across a **stream**. Wind beyond through trees to a fork and choose the right branch, signposted to 'Sheepdip'. Shortly cross a **second bridge** and carry on beside the stream, before long arriving at yet another fork. Keep ahead, still following signs to 'Sheepdip'. Breaking to the edge of the **wood**, walk on at the foot of steeply sloping grassland. Slipping back into the trees, walk on to a **4-way signpost**.

The woodland of the Ludon valley is a dramatic contrast to the windblown starkness of the coastal cliffs. Sheltered from the worst of the elements, native ash and oak grow tall, hazel and holly expand into portly bushes and willow thrives beside the stream that squirms along

the valley floor. In spring, East Wood is one of the best places in the area to see carpets of bluebells, which seize their moment of glory before the trees gain full leaf and cut out the sunlight. Spring too is the best time for birds, although you may only hear their song as they mark out territory and advertise for mates. But with luck you might spot a willow warbler or pied flycatcher.

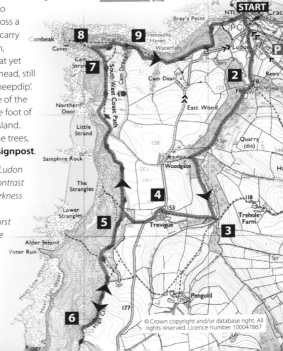

© Crown copyright and/or database right. All rights reserved. Licence number 100047867

Looking back along the coast to Cambeak

3. Turn right, the way signed to 'Trevigue', and climb to a kissing gate at the edge of the wood. Bear left, straight up the hillside, *lovely views opening as you gain height*. Through a gate, carry on along a grass path, making for a small gate at the top corner of the field. Walk out past the front of **Trevigue** onto the lane.

4. Head left along the lane for some 200 metres before leaving through a small gate on the right onto the National Trust's land above **The Strangles**. Walk a short distance to a fork and bear left to meet the **South West Coast Path**.

5. Head left, passing a steep path to the beach far below and climb onto **High Cliff** just over 1 kilometre away. *At 223 metres above sea level, it is the highest and one of the most dramatic points along Cornwall's north coast.*

6. After enjoying the view, retrace your steps and continue past **Point 5**. The path falls easily along the edge of the steeply sloping cliff above **The Strangles**, before dropping more determinedly into a side valley behind **Little Strand**. Climb out beyond and carry on, soon gently descending again to a junction at the base of **Cambeak**.

Sunset at the natural sea arch on The Strangles' rocky shore

7. The paths off right bypass the headland along **Cam Draught**, but you should stick with the **Coast Path**, which climbs left. Carry on past a waypost to a stunning **viewpoint on the top of Cambeak**.

8. Head back to the waypost and now branch left, losing height ever more steeply off the grassy top along the northern flank of the point. Lower down, zigzags help ease the gradient and open more views of the cliffs.

The **Cam Draught** paths join below the zigzags, the way dropping to cross a **stream** at the base of the valley.

9. There's another sharp but short pull before the path undulates on behind the lower cliffs of **Tremoutha Haven**.

Amongst the rocks below the path at Tremoutha Haven are the remains of a wartime German Schnellboot, a fast torpedo boat which could reach almost 40 knots. Surrendered to the British Navy at the end of the war in 1945, it was being towed around the coast to Pembrokeshire for use as a gunnery training target. However, the hawser parted in heavy seas and S89 drifted ashore. Deteriorating weather prevented its recovery and the storm drove the boat hard onto the rocks where it eventually broke up.

Keep going with the **Coast Path**, eventually dropping from the cliffs to pass t**ennis courts**.

Keep going to the head of the bay, there meeting the lane at **Crackington Haven**, opposite the car park, to complete the walk. ◆

The 'Crackington formation'
The cliffs either side of Crackington Haven are composed of multi-layered sandstones and shales. They were laid down in tropical waters some 300 million years ago, the landmasses of Armorica (France) and Avalonia (England and Wales) coming together, crumpling, lifting and fracturing the strata in the process. Erosion has revealed remarkable multi-folding and fracturing in the cliffs while wave-cut beaches slice through the grain of the upended layers.

High summer lights the breakwater at the entrance to Port Isaac

Port Quin & Port Isaac

An energetic cliff-top ramble links two of north Cornwall's most attractive coastal villages

What to expect:
Good paths but with some steep ascents

Distance/Time: 8.5 kilometres/ 5¼ miles. Allow 3 to 3½ hours

Start: Port Quin National Trust car park (pay and display)

Grid ref: SW 971 804

Ordnance Survey map: Explorer 106: Newquay and Padstow

Refreshment: The Salt Pig food van, Port Quin car park OR The Golden Lion, Port Isaac | 01208 880336 | www.thegoldenlionportisaac.co.uk

Walk Outline

Leaving Port Quin, the route runs overland across Roscarrock Hill, dipping in and out of the narrow valley behind Pine Haven before dropping to Port Isaac. Having explored the old village, where a pub lies behind the harbour, it is a strenuous climb around Lobber Point into Pine Haven. Steep ups and downs take the path around Varley Head, behind Downgate Cove and onto Kellan Head, the way finally turning the point for a more gentle finish beside the cove back to Port Quin.

Port Quin

Today's handful of harbour cottages belies Port Quin's former busyness as a medieval port, when plentiful pilchard and herring were landed to be salted for export. Ships came and went with cargoes of coal, salt, farm goods and stone as well as lead, antimony, silver and copper, dug from local mines that exploited rich ore seams running along the coast. But the population fell during the mid-19th century after fish stocks declined and the new railways took away the centuries-old trade of coastal shipping.

Lobster pots, Port Isaac

Live lobsters are blue

Local fishing boats moored in Port Isaac's natural harbour

The Walk

1. Leaving the **car park**, follow the lane to the right. After 150 metres, at a bend, branch up left past the front of **cottages** to find a **stone stile** beside a field gate. Walk ahead, passing a gnarled and twisted sycamore tree, to keep an old hedge on your right.

2. Entering the next field, bear away from the hedge, slanting across the slope of the hill to a pair of gates on the far boundary. Cross a stile between them and carry on along a field track. Keep going from field to field, shortly cresting the rise to gain a view of Port Isaac.

3. Through a gate, leave the track as it swings right to **Roscarrock Farm**.

An established manor comprising 13 households when recorded by William's commissioners in his Great Domesday Survey of 1086, Roscarrock is one of the oldest farming settlements in Cornwall. The present manor house dates from the end of the 15th century and was built by the Roscarrocks, one of whose ancestors was elected MP for Cornwall in 1347 and a descendant twice served as Sheriff in the 16th century.

A fine example of its type, the house

encloses a courtyard and had its own chapel. The family retained its Catholic allegiance during Elizabeth I's reign, with Nicholas Roscarrock suffering imprisonment in the Tower and racking for his support of the priesthood and non attendance at church. He survived the ordeal and went on to write a history of the lives of Cornish saints. The family died out in the 1670s and the manor has been held by only three other families since.

Walk downhill beside a hedge towards the coast. Turn within the bottom corner and carry on to find a redundant stile on the left. A path slopes down across the steep bracken and shrub of the valley side into trees at the bottom. Cross a **bridge** to a stile and junction of paths. Take the one ahead up the opposite side of the valley. Breaking from scrub into a

field, a **waymark** directs you ahead, past a **rocket post** and on over the crest to a stile in the far field bank. Continue beside the left hedge, ultimately dropping out onto a street above **Port Isaac**. Head down the hill into the **village** where, just beyond the **harbour**, you will find **The Golden Lion**.

By the 16th century, when the pier was built, Port Isaac was already a thriving port, trading along the coast and across the Channel. Its fishing fleet once numbered 50 boats, bringing home pilchard to be cleaned and salted in fish cellars, one of which survives as the fish market.

Appearance in films and TV series, including the original Poldark and Doc Martin have boosted the village's fame and it is renowned for one of the narrowest streets in the country, known as Squeezy Belly Alley, which lies opposite the Golden Lion.

© Crown copyright and/or database right. All rights reserved. Licence number 100047867

Port Quin seems quiet compared to the bustle of nearby Port Isaac

4. When you've had a wander round, head back up the way you came and carry on to the top of the street.

5. Now turn right beside the entrance to houses to pick up the ongoing **South West Coast Path**. The switchback mood of the return is immediately set with a steep pull up steps before curving around **Lobber Point**. It's then immediately downhill to **Pine Haven** followed by another strenuous climb to the headland beyond. The path continues its rollercoaster course to **Varley Head**, where the main path cuts across the neck. However, the lower path reveals more fantastic views.

6. Carry on with the **Coast Path** above **Greengarden and Downgate coves**, taking advantage of frequent pauses to admire the views behind which are equally splendid. Although not Cornwall's highest cliffs, they are amongst its most spectacular. Keep going, eventually rounding **Kellan Head** where a **bench** makes a fine spot for a picnic.

In 1816 a Dutch sloop bound for Amsterdam laden with wool, foundered on the rocks below. All the crew were lost as the ship broke up, but the cargo washed ashore, including some chests of coins, which were swiftly 'salvaged' by the villagers.

7. The ups and downs continue until you finally turn the point sheltering **Port Quin**. *Just across the water is* **Doyden Castle**, *while further along the coast to the west is Rumps Point and its offshore rocks, The Mouls.*

The path now falls gently beside the inlet to **Port Quin**, dropping behind **cottages** to the **harbour** and out to the main lane and **car park** to complete the walk. ♦

Doyden Castle

Overlooking the mouth of Port Quin is the crenellated Doyden Castle. Built in 1830, it was the merrymaking retreat of a wealthy and somewhat infamous Wadebridge merchant, who used it as an impressive venue for lavish parties to indulge his good-living passions of food, wine and gambling. The Victorian Gothic lodge has only a single room on each floor, built over a copious wine cellar, but commands superb views across the bay. .

A surfer on Polzeath's beach at dusk, silhouetted against Pentire Point

Pentire Point

An impressive headland walk with stunning cliff-top scenery overlooking a fine surfing beach

What to expect:
Good paths and tracks with some steady ascents

Distance/Time: 10 kilometres/ 6¼ miles. Allow 3½ to 4 hours

Start: Lundy Bay National Trust car park

Grid ref: SW 952 794

Ordnance Survey map: Explorer 111: Bude, Boscastle & Tintagel

Refreshment: The Waterfront, Polzeath | 01208 869655 | www.waterfrontpolzeath.co.uk OR Granny's Café, Polzeath

Walk Outline

The first leg skirts flower meadows to the hamlet of Pentireglaze and follows a valley fold to the sea at Hayle Bay. The way then takes to the cliffs, undulating upward to Pentire Point. It continues above high cliffs before dropping across a narrow neck onto The Rumps. The ongoing path rises and falls above successive coves to Lundy Hole, where there's an impressive collapsed cave and sheltered beach. The return rises along a wooded valley back to the car park.

Pentire Lead Mines

Lead was mined on the Pentire peninsula for at least 300 years until the latter part of the 19th century. Two separate lodes were worked, producing ores that also contained antimony and silver. Antimony, used by the ancient Egyptians as a cosmetic and medicine, hardens certain alloys and a range of applications from engine parts to bells were developed. In 1784 Henry Shrapnel alloyed it with lead and developed an anti-personnel shell that ejected multiple bullets. Pentire's ore was rich and yielded nearly 1,000 tons of lead, but around half a ton of silver was also extracte — a not insignificant amount.

Lifeguard, Polzeath

Bottlenose dolphins

The Walk

1. Going left from the **Lundy Bay car park**, cross to find a permissive path leaving through a field gate, a few metres along on the right. Stick with left hedge beside the lane, passing through a kissing gate into the next meadow, turn right away from the road. In the next corner, swing left and then keep ahead with the ongoing track to emerge at the corner of a lane.

2. Walk forward to a junction by **cottages** at **Pentireglaze**. Wind down to the left, looking for a gated path beyond the buildings signed off right to 'Pentireglaze Haven'. Carry on as it opens to fields, eventually reaching the bend of

a track. Take the right branch, which leads down to **Pentireglaze Haven**.

3. Follow the **Coast Path** right behind the **beach**, crossing a **stream** and slanting onto the **headland** beyond. The increasing height opens a view across to the surfing beach of Hayle Bay. The onward path undulates above a rocky shore, before a final steeper pull up to **Pentire Point**.

The small island off the point is Newland, while further around, behind the Rump, is The Mouls. They are the last strongholds for breeding puffins along this coast. Puffins spend most of their lives at sea, only returning to their colonies around April to breed. These loveable birds nest in burrows, sometimes using those abandoned by rabbits or Manx shearwaters and, safe from land-based predators such as foxes or rats, these tiny islets are ideal. The parents share incubation and feeding but then leave en masse, abandoning the chicks to find their

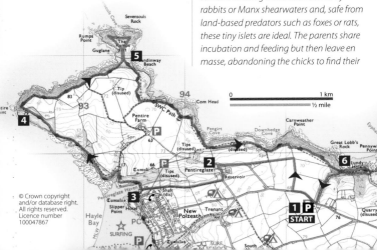

© Crown copyright and/or database right. All rights reserved. Licence number 100047867

A large sea cave at Pentire Point

own way to the sea. Although puffins can live for 20 years, they only reach breeding maturity after five or six years and lay only one egg each year.

4. Turning the corner, the path rises and falls across green, steeply sloping cliffs, the view now to **The Rumps headland**.

Look out for a plaque beside the path which commemorates Laurence Binyon's poem 'For The Fallen', which he wrote here in 1914, just after the outbreak of the First World War as the whole country reeled at the massive loss of life sustained during the first battles that took place in France. It was published in September of that year in The Times, and the fourth verse, recorded on the plaque, is often recited at Remembrance Services.

Closer to, the **Iron Age banks and ditches** across the neck of the headland can be clearly seen. As the way then forks, keep left dropping to the outer embankment, where a gap takes the path through the defences to explore the dramatic cliff-top scenery of the twin promontories.

The Rumps owe their curious shape to the relative hardness of the volcanic basalt rock from which they are formed.

The Rumps headland, near Pentire Point, is excellent for sea watching

Connected to the rest of the headland by a narrow isthmus, it made an ideal defensible site. The inner pair of ramparts date from around the 2nd century BC with the third being added somewhat later. It is a sophisticated construction with the banks being faced in stone, while the outer defence was possibly topped with a wooden palisade. It appears to have been occupied for around 300 years until the Romans arrived. Traces of roundhouses have been identified within the enclosure as well as pottery and stone artefacts such as spindle whorls used for spinning wool and querns for grinding grain.

5. Returning to the ramparts, now bear left with the **Coast Path**. Continue above a succession of **coves** around the coast, later passing the fenced off **shafts of old lead mines**. Eventually, past **Carnweather Point** and **Great Lobb's Rock**, the way drops along a hedged path to a junction above the corner of **Lundy Bay**.

6. Take the left branch, and where it then forks, keep left again with the **Coast Path**. It runs across the slope of a ridge behind the cliffs, shortly leading to an impressive crater, **Lundy Hole**, into which the sea surges at high tide through a l**arge cave**. Just beyond, the path drops to another junction above the

small cove of **Lundy Bay**, where there is access to the beach.

7. Turn around to head back, branching left on a lower path beside the ridge. The paths come together and return you to the junction at **Point 6**. Now turn left on a National Trust path, signed to the 'Car Park', which climbs along a valley to come out opposite the **Lundy Bay car park** to complete the walk. ◆

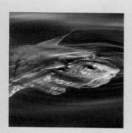

Sea watching

Projecting into the sea, The Rumps is a great place for sea watching. Dolphins and porpoise are regulars, but basking sharks and even a killer whale have been spotted too. Another unusual passer-by is the massive ocean sunfish, whose flattened body appears all head and can grow to over 3 metres, weighing in at nearly one tonne. Although a deepwater swimmer it sometimes tips on its side to bask at the surface on sunny days.

Trevose Head Lighthouse's white paint is bright under the summer sun

Trevose Head

A superb coast walk past a lighthouse and three fine beaches

What to expect:
Good paths and generally steady climbs

Distance/Time: 10 kilometres/ 6 miles. Allow 3 to 3½ hours

Start: Harlyn Bridge car park (pay and display)

Grid ref: SW 879 754

Ordnance Survey map: Explorer 106: Newquay & Padstow

Refreshment: The Harlyn Inn | 01841 520207 | www.harlyninn.com

Walk Outline

Lane and path take the way across the neck of the Trevose peninsula past Harlyn House to the Trevose Golf Club. A path traces the edge of the course to the coastal dunes, down to the beach. The Coast Path initially follows the tide line before climbing onto low cliffs, which later gain height to an old quarry facing Dinas Head. Passing behind the lighthouse, the way rounds the headland, drops above the lifeboat station, and runs over low cliffs behind sandy bays back to Harlyn.

Mother Ivey

Mother Ivey was a 16th-century white witch: probably the local midwife with enough herbal knowledge to act as doctor too. One year when times were hard, a shipment of dried fish came back from the Mediterranean unsold and Mother Ivey pleaded with the merchant to let the villagers have them. Instead he ploughed them into one of his fields as fertiliser. It's said she cursed the land: 'If ever the soil is broken, death will follow'. Soon after, the merchant's son was thrown from his horse and died in the field. In recent times, a detectorist and a water board official have both suffered fatal heart attacks there.

Trevose Head Lighthouse

Kestrel on the cliffs

The Walk

1. Out of the car park go down the hill and continue past **The Harlyn Inn**. After 400 metres, turn off right onto **Sandy Lane**. At a footpath sign, just before a gateway, leave along a track on the left. Over a stile, walk on at the edge of and then across a field to emerge onto a lane. Cross to a gap opposite and go right along a gravel drive. Immediately beyond a gateway, branch off right with a footpath into trees past **Harlyn House**.

At the end, turn out right through a gate back onto the lane.

2. Walk left and follow the lane on for just over 1 kilometre, eventually winding past a **car park** and up to a junction by **Trevose Golf Club**.

3. Turn off sharp right through a kissing gate on an enclosed path that runs between the car park and adjacent houses. Keep going as it later passes through trees and eventually comes to the edge of **sand dunes**. Maintain your direction to emerge on the beach at **Constantine Bay**.

© Crown copyright and/or database right. All rights reserved. Licence number 100047867

Harlyn Bay's big swells draw late-season surfers to North Cornwall

4. Walk right to follow the **South West Coast Path** along the high water line. At the far end of the beach, climb away up **steps** to continue along the top of a low, sandy cliff above a rocky shore. Further on, the path splits either side of a massive crater, called simply **Round Hole**. Unseen from the seaward side path is a massive **cave**, which connects it to the open sea.

Such holes are formed as wave action exploits weaknesses in the cliff to create a littoral cave. The hydraulic force of the water, aided by the abrasive power of the sand and pebbles it carries, creates an ever-growing chamber, which can then collapse to leave a massive crater.

5. Just beyond, a path leaves left onto the jutting promontory of **Dinas Head**. However, the route continues ahead across the neck and past an **old quarry floor**.

The headland is a spectacular place for wild flowers. Amongst the less common species to be found are golden samphire, shore dock, rock sea-lavender and wild asparagus. Have a look too at the traditional herringbone stone walls where lichen and ferns grow.

Constantine Bay's broad sands are rightly popular with surfers

Climb steps onto a track, which leads to **Trevose Head Lighthouse**. Follow it briefly left before leaving up to the right. The path curves round above the lighthouse across the headland, bending right again above **Cat's Cove**. A path then branches off left to a viewpoint behind Merope Rocks, swinging back to meet the **Coast Path** at a kissing gate.

6. Cross a track serving the **lifeboat station** to another gate opposite.

Padstow's first lifeboat was established around 1825 by the Harbour Association. It was based in Hawker's Cove at the mouth of the River Camel, 4 miles to the east, with

a second station being added in 1899. It moved here in 1967 because of silting in the river mouth, with the new lifeboat house being opened in 2006 to accommodate the new Tamar Class boat, Spirit of Padstow.

A contained path runs on behind cliff-top developments, emerging onto a narrow drive. The path continues opposite, shortly regaining the cliff before winding past a **cottage** to another track, where there is access to the beach. Keep with the **Coast Path** through the gate opposite, soon meeting a surfaced path from a **caravan site**.

7. Follow it briefly left then branch off

right up steps. Carry on along the coast out to **Cataclews Point**, the path then sweeping back to run on behind **Harlyn Bay**. Eventually, the path turns down to the sands, to continue above the high water mark. At the far end of the beach, turn up beside a **stream** to a lane. The **car park** is then a short walk up to the left, and completes the walk. ♦

Prehistoric finds

The fields behind Harlyn Bay have been identified as a Bronze Age cemetery. More than 200 graves have been found containing grave goods including jewellery, tools and loom weights. Of particular interest are two lunulae unearthered by a labourer in 1865. Wafer-thin, crescent shaped neck ornaments, they are made from Irish gold. A similar discovery in Brittany has identical tooling marks, suggesting they were made by the same craftsman.

Bedruthan Steps is named after the isolated rock stacks below the cliffs

Bedruthan Steps

Rock towers, stacks and vertical cliffs add drama to one of north Cornwall's finest beaches

What to expect:
Coast paths with some steeper climbs, long flight of steps to the beach

Distance/Time: 6.5 kilometres/ 4 miles. Allow 2½ to 3 hours

Start: Carnewas National Trust car park at Bedruthan (pay and display)

Grid ref: SW 849 689

Ordnance Survey map: Explorer 106: Newquay & Padstow

Refreshment: Carnewas Tea Room at car park | 01637 860701 | www.carnewas-tea-rooms.co.uk

Walk Outline

From the car park, the route follows the cliffs north for 1.6km above the Bedruthan and Pentire Steps. It then loops inland past Pentire Farm, dropping into the valley beyond. A wetland nature reserve takes the path to the coast at Porth Mear. After a steep climb to regain the cliffs, the way passes behind a succession of rocky coves to round Park Head. With the height now recovered it is an easy walk back above Bedruthan.

Bedruthan Steps

The only access to the beach is a dizzyingly steep staircase, cut by 19th-century miners, who worked adits at the base of the cliffs for lead, silver and antimony. Although the workings were abandoned in 1874, horse drawn carriages brought day trippers from Newquay to this stunning bay, where the line of cliffs is in constant retreat from the face of the incessant surge of waves that undercut and exploit any weakness. Monoliths of harder rock are left as isolated stacks; and an air of romanticism was added with the tale that they were stepping stones laid down by the giant Bedruthan.

Cave at Bedruthan

Fulmar

The Walk

1. Head towards the coast from the **car park,** taking the right branch where the path forks. *Almost immediately there are views along the coast past Park Head to the lighthouse on Trevose Head.* Joining the **South West Coast Path**, follow it right to descend a flight of **stone steps**. At the bottom, drop left to a **viewpoint** where you will find a steep **staircase of 120 steps** down the cliff to **Bedruthan beach**. If you venture down, be aware that the beach is covered at high tide.

2. Regaining the **Coast Path**, carry on north, shortly passing **Diggory's Island**, a massive stack. The small beach beyond is known as **Pentire Steps**, above which the path swings behind a short length of wall. Through a kissing gate at the end head on across grass to the cliff top at the far end of Pentire Steps. There is access to the beach here too, a path off sharp left that drops steeply across the sloping cliff. However, it's not suitable for everyone as it requires something of a scramble towards the bottom.

3. The onward route is through a kissing gate on the right, along a path signed to a 'car park'. Walk away at the field edge before leaving, partway along the third field, through a small gate on the right (not the adjacent field gate). A contained path leads to the **Park Head car park**.

4. Follow a track away to the left,

abandoning it just before reaching **cottages**, through the second of two adjacent gates on the right. Walk on by the left wall to a corner and there bear half-left towards a gap in the hedge. A trod heads down across the slope into the base of the valley. Through a kissing gate, keep going across a **wetland**

© Crown copyright and/or database right. All rights reserved. Licence number 100047867

Sea mist veils the rock stacks below the Bedruthan cliffs

nature area. *The boat 'wreckage' passed a little further on is not a beached relic from when the creek might have been navigable, but an art work.* Approaching the coast, bear right at a fork and swing over a **bridge** to reach a **sheltered rocky cove** where there are good rock pools.

5. Return across the bridge and now turn right. The **Coast Path** climbs on towards Park Head, cutting behind successive promontories and then **Park Head** itself, *where there are the embankments of an ancient promontory fort.* The way eventually meets your outward route above **Pentire Steps**. Retrace your steps back to the **car park**, enjoying the views again from a different perspective of compass, tide and light, to complete the walk. ♦

Underwater marvels

Rock pools are a great place to glimpse life beneath the sea. Some creatures like colourful anemones make them their permanent home, clinging to the rocks and catching food with stinging tentacles. Others are washed in by the tide and small fish and prawns can often be seen swimming about. Crabs like to hide in crevices or beneath rocks, their pincers ready to grab a passing fish. There may be shrimps too, but they like to burrow into sand.

Approaching Holywell Bay from Kelsey Head on the South West Coast Path

Holywell & Kelsey Head

Expansive beaches, rolling sand dunes and flower-rich grasslands are another aspect of Cornwall's north coast

Distance/Time: 8 kilometres/ 5 miles. Allow 2½ to 3 hours

Start: Holywell Bay National Trust car park (pay and display)

Grid ref: SW 767 587

Ordnance Survey map: Explorer 104: Redruth & St Agnes

Refreshment: St Pirans Inn, Holywell | 01637 830205 | www.stpiransinn.com OR Bowgie Inn, West Pentire | 01637 830363 | www.bowgie.com

Walk Outline

Skirting Holywell, the walk takes to the edge of the dunes before crossing the sandy grasslands of The Kelseys and Cubert Common into the Treago valley. There's another climb over West Pentire , the route then dropping to the Coast Path above Crantock Beach. The way back follows the cliffs around Pentire Point West into Porth Joke before rising again onto Kelsey Head. The final stretch lies above Holywell Beach and across the dunes behind back to the car park.

The Poppies of Pentire

Stubble grazing and spring sowing across West Pentire's small fields encourages wildflowers. A late spring delight is a mist of red of poppies amidst the corn. Prolific flowerers and propagators, their seed can lie dormant for years before sprouting when the ground is disturbed, as were the Flanders fields during the Great War. Also seen is the once-common corn marigold. Ground-nesting corn buntings are returning too and farmers are encouraged to sow cereals thickly in the middle of fields to help protect nests from predators. A thin winter-sown crop ensures food throughout the year.

Poppies above Porth Joke

Corn bunting

The Walk

1. Out of the **car park**, turn right past **St Pirans Inn**. Where the lane then bends, leave left along a narrow lane. Keep ahead past a junction and then bear off right at a footpath sign onto the edge of dunes. Curving right behind houses, disregard a path off left and stick with the periphery, walking through bushes and along a **grassy gully**. Passing through trees a path joins from the right near a short length of wooden fence. As the way then rises onto the **dunes**, keep by the right-hand fence alongside a **golf course**.

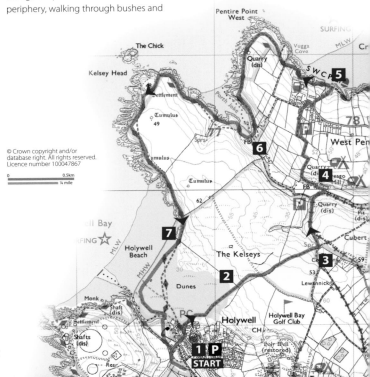

© Crown copyright and/or database right. All rights reserved. Licence number 100047867

Overlooking Holywell Bay with Kelsey Head rising at the far end

2. Cresting the rise, pass through a kissing gate onto **open grassland**, the way ahead signed to 'Crantock'. Shortly meeting a crossing track, slip through the gate to continue on the opposite side of the fence. Where the fence then turns away, keep ahead to a fingerpost.

3. Swing left towards West Pentire and Porth Joke, falling to join a track that leads on down the **valley**. At the bottom, curve right past a **car park** to the **Polly Joke Campsite**.

Porth (or Polly) Joke is a beautifully sandy inlet, well sheltered from the breeze. Its peculiar name derives from an Anglicisation of the Cornish Porth Lojowek, meaning a richly vegetated cove.

Turn off left through a kissing gate beside its entrance onto a contained path. Swing over a **bridge** to meet a track by **Treago Mill**.

4. To the left the track angles up between field boundaries, the gradient easing as it eventually crests the hill. Reaching a T-junction, go right to a small green overlooked by the **Bowgie Inn**. Bear right and left to follow a drive beside **Crantock Bay Apartments**. Becoming a path, it

The extensive, mature dune system behind Holywell Bay

drops to meet the coast above **Crantock Beach**. Facing the Atlantic rollers, it is a popular surfing spot.

5. The way lies to the left, undulating towards Pentire Point West. At a junction above **Vugga Cove**, go right through a kissing gate. The way shortly splits into high and low paths around the point. The lower one passes an impressive **collapsed sea cave** near the tip. Carry on, in time curving in above **Porth Joke** and descending to the head of the inlet.

6. Crossing a **stream**, the **Coast Path** rises onto the next **headland**. Reaching **Kelsey Head** the path runs beside the prominent bank of an **Iron Age settlement** and there are views to The Chick lying off the point. The cliffs turn in again above the northern end of **Holywell Beach**, eventually passing through a kissing gate at the edge of the **dune system**.

7. Make your way onto the **beach** (it offers easier walking than the dunes).

A cave in the southern cliffs of Kelsey Head contains a series of natural basins that fill with water seeping from the rock, where mothers once immersed their sick children, believing that the spring had healing properties.

Towards the far end of the sand, turn up beside a **stream** running across the sand. Leaving the beach, continue along a path, shortly joined by another one from the **dunes**.

Cross a **bridge** and walk on to emerge on the lane beside **St Pirans Inn**. The car park is then just to the right, to complete the walk. ♦

Dunes and maritime grasslands

Although Holywell's dunes are dominated by marram grass, other plants such as sea holly are abundant too. The younger dunes shelter the stabilised grasslands of the Kelseys and Cubert Common, whose calcareous soils favour wildflowers including pyramidal orchid and cowslip. Insects to look out for include great green bush crickets and dark green fritillary butterflies, while amongst the birds to be seen are skylark and wheatear.

The iconic Towanroath Engine House at Wheal Coates tin mine

St Agnes Head

*Impressive tin mining relics and a grand view of the coast
from St Agnes Beacon*

What to expect:
*Good paths and tracks,
steady climbs*

Distance/Time: 11 kilometres/ 7 miles. Allow 4 to 4½ hours

Start: Chapel Porth National Trust car park (pay and display)

Grid ref: SW 697 494

Ordnance Survey map: Explorer 104 Redruth & St Agnes

Refreshment: Chapel Porth Beach Café | 01872 552487 |
www.nationaltrust.org.uk

Walk Outline

*Leaving the beach at Chapel Porth, the first leg rises
along coastal cliffs past the impressive ruins of the Wheal
Coates mine. The way continues easily below the National
Coastwatch station on St Agnes Head, rounding the point
before climbing from the coast and on over the summit of St
Agnes Beacon. Falling beyond to Goonvrea, the route drops
past more abandoned workings along a shady valley before
following Chapel Combe back to the sea.*

Poldark Country

Two BBC television adaptations of Winston Graham's
Poldark novels have made extensive use of the Cornish
coast and countryside as settings, and have done much to
champion the natural beauty and industrial heritage of the
county. Stirring the public imagination, the most recent
adaptation used over 15 different locations. Botallack and
Levant featured as the main mining sites and Gunwalloe
saw booty being taken from a wreck. Also used were the
cliffs at Park Head, the beach at Hollywell and Kynance
Cove, while Charlestown near St Austell doubled for Truro.

Wheal Coates ruins

Chough

The Walk

1. Leaving the **car park**, head back up the lane. After a few metres, double back left with the **South West Coast Path**. Climb away above the beach, keeping right with the main path above a fold. At a junction higher up, turn sharp left across the fold. Go forward at the next crossing path to rise more easily across the heather-clad cliff. Appearing ahead is the **Towanroath Engine House,** which pumped water from the adjacent shaft.

The coast between Chapel Porth and St Agnes Head bears the ruins and scars of extensive mining during the 19th century, when Wheal Coates and neighbouring mines produced both tin and copper. To the non-Cornish, the term wheal *has generally become synonymous with mine but in fact, it simply means a place of work, which is what the mines were. And despite the often romantic suffixes which many mines bear, the work was hard and dangerous, even for the children and women employed above ground.*

2. Walk on past the impressive **chimney**, forking right and then left at successive junctions. Reaching the top, bear left beside a wall, shortly passing a **fenced-off shaft** on your left. Keep left with the **Coast Path** to a viewpoint above **Carn Gowla** and carry on with the cliff-top path to **St Agnes Head**.

0   0.5km
⅓ mile

© Crown copyright and/ or database right. All rights reserved. Licence number 100047867

The South West Coast Path near Chapel Porth, looking towards Wheal Coates

3. A path up right leads to a **National Coastwatch station**, but the onward route continues around the coast. After 600 metres, watch for a **waymark** post and then, very soon after, a narrow path climbing off right.

4. Head up, passing another **mine shaft** half-hidden by the heather, to a junction.

The metal lattice cages dotted about the heath cover abandoned mine shafts and serve a dual purpose; preventing people and animals falling in (the shafts can be very deep), while allowing the bats that live there to freely come and go.

Britain has some 17 different species, of which 12 breed in Cornwall, but numbers have significantly declined over the last century and all are now protected. Traditional roosts are caves, old buildings and hollow trees, but old mines and stone quarries serve equally well. Bats are perhaps best seen as they emerge at dusk to feed on flying insects. Particularly rare is the greater horseshoe bat, so named because of an oddly-shaped nose leaf, which helps its echolocation. With a wingspan of around 40 centimetres, it is Britain's largest bat.

Coastal heathland above Wheal Coates tin mine ruins

Keep with the track ahead over a **boundary bank**. As it then swings right, go forward past a **barrier**, another track soon joining from the left. Carry on between fields, eventually coming out onto a lane.

5. Go right and almost immediately bear off left on a rising path onto **St Agnes Beacon**. Ignore crossing paths and take either branch at a fork shortly after, continuing upwards to reach the **trig column turned topograph** marking the hill's summit, a superb viewpoint.

6. Carry on ahead beyond the summit, choosing the right branch where the path then splits. Lower down, go over a crossing path, but then almost immediately, fork right, heading towards a gate.

However, where the path splits again, bear left, walking down to meet a track. Follow it right to emerge onto a lane at **Goonvrea**.

7. Turn left, but leave after a few metres for a bridleway signed off on the right. Drop to another lane and continue along the track opposite signed to 'Chapel Porth and Mingoose'.

Where the way forks, bear left, but at a second fork just after, keep right. Through a kissing gate, turn right on a contained

path along the valley. Further down, wind across the stream and through a gateway, walking ahead to join a track. At the bottom, ignore a drive off right and cross a **stream** to meet a T-junction.

8. Turn right on a bridleway along the fold of **Chapel Combe**, passing more **derelict mine buildings** and spoil heaps. At the bottom, cross a **bridge** back to the **car park** to complete the walk. ♦

St Agnes Beacon

Rising 192 metres above sea level, St Agnes Beacon is the highest point for miles around with unrivalled views over the surrounding countryside. It has been the site of a beacon watchtower since at least the 18th century and was part of the country's early warning system against Napoleonic invasion during the 19th century. No longer used by the Ordnance Survey, the summit trig point has been remodelled as a topograph showing surrounding points of interest.

Spectacular cliffs overlooking the Crane Islands

Reskajeage Downs

An undemanding walk along impressive cliffs and through the Tehidy valley nature reserve

What to expect:
Woodland and cliff-top paths, no dogs allowed in nature reserve

Distance/Time: 9.5 kilometres/ 6 miles. Allow 3 to 3½ hours

Start: North Cliffs National Trust car park

Grid ref: SW 618 428

Ordnance Survey map: Explorer 104 Redruth & St Agnes

Refreshment: Visitor Centre Café, Tehidy Country Park

Walk Outline

Following a short walk along the cliff top, the way drops around fields into the Red River valley. After briefly following a lane, it rises along a wooded fold into the Tehidy Estate. Crossing the stream into Oak Wood, it continues past Otter Bridge and around a reed-edged lake to the Visitor Centre. The route winds on through North Cliff Plantation before regaining the coast above Basset's Cove. The final stretch is along spectacular cliffs at the edge of the down.

The Bassets of Tehidy

The Bassets came to Tehidy in the middle of the 12th century and held the manor alongside extensive estates elsewhere in Cornwall and in Devon. Much of their wealth derived from mining and Tehidy itself, which was centred on a succession of grand mansions. With the decline in mining, the Bassets sold the estate in 1915, with the main house becoming a sanatorium. Although rebuilt after a fire, the hospital finally closed in 1988. However, the hall survives in a private enclave as up-market housing while the surrounding woodland is managed as a country park.

Tehidy Country Park

Grey seal

Bluebell woods on the Tehidy Estate in spring

The Walk

1. Head east along the **Coast Path** from the back of the **car park** for 800 metres, passing two more small car parks before reaching a third.

The Bassets' wealth may well have come from mining, but they didn't necessarily want it in their own back yard. Around 1825, lodes of lead, silver and zinc were discovered in the cliffs back towards Navax Point, but mining licences were granted only on condition that 'no disturbance of land was made inland from the cliffs.' Consequently the deposits

were worked from the beach or cliff face terraces.

2. Leave the coast and follow the access track to the lane. Cross to a gap opposite and stride away at the field edge. Carry on beside subsequent fields and then down a steeper wooded path, ultimately emerging onto a lane.

3. Turn left, walking down to a bend, where a track leaves left into the woods of **Tehidy Country Park**. After 800 metres, look for a path off right down steps signed 'Oak Wood and Otter Bridge'.

4. Drop to **Snake Bridge**, crossing a couple of **streams** and then a **boardwalk**, rising beyond to a broader path. Follow it left through **Oak Wood**, soon merging with another path from the right, Keep going, another path eventually joining as

you approach a signposted junction by **Otter Bridge** near the **ruin** of a former mill.

5. Remaining on this bank, take the path off right (NO DOGS) signed 'South Drive and Lakes Visitor Centre'. Keep left at a subsequent fork and disregard a later bridge, shortly reaching the **lake**. Carry on around its southern bank to a **bridge** at the head of the lake. Ignore that and instead veer right upstream to cross by a **second bridge**, the path soon leading to a **car park**. Bear left past it to reach the **Visitor Centre and Café**.

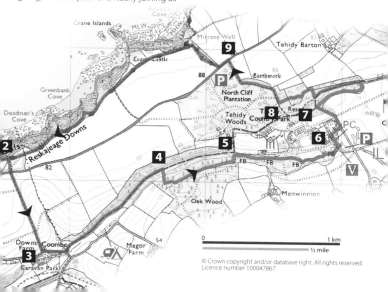

© Crown copyright and/or database right. All rights reserved.
Licence number 100047867

Low tide at Basset's Cove and the Crane Islands

6. Keep with the ongoing path past the Visitor Centre to a junction and turn right, the way signed to 'North Cliff Plantation and East Lodge'. At a meeting of drives take the one ahead between a **golf course** and houses. Where that then swings left, keep ahead through a kissing gate along a woodland path. Leave at the far end through a second gate to a crossing path.

7. The route lies right, marked 'East Lodge'. Reaching another junction by a bench, walk left, the way signed towards 'North Cliff and Coombe'. At the next junction, go right (marked as the Country Park red route), soon swinging left past the site of the **Tehidy Temple.** *The building was constructed as a summer house with a view to the now demolished mansion.*

8. At the next junction, turn right, staying with the red route past another junction a few metres along. Reaching a crosspath, walk ahead right (not sharp right) to leave the woods. A contained path runs beside a field to meet a lane.

9. Go left but after a few metres, turn off along a track on the right that leads to a **coastal car park** above **Basset's Cove**. The steep path behind the car park down to the beach necessitates a scramble and is not recommended. The way back is to the left along the **Coast Path**.

Ongoing coastal erosion is revealed at Crane Castle, where a cliff-top section of double rampart and ditch is all that remains of a once extensive Iron Age promontory fort largely lost to the sea. The fort is thought to have covered around five hectares, extending

over what are now the offshore Crane Islands. A pottery shard, part of a flask from Gaul, dates the site to around 100AD.

Continue along the coast back to the car park to complete the walk. ♦

Tehidy Country Park

The country park is a great place to see wildlife. In spring, keep an ear open for the great spotted woodpecker. Its distinctive drumming may be it excavating a nest hole in a tree trunk or simply marking territory and advertising for a mate. Easily recognised, it is a medium sized black and white bird with a distinctive red rump patch, with males having also a flash of red on the nape.

Carn Galver's ruined engine house above Porthmoina Cove

Carn Galver

Remnants of the tin industry and a wild coast, returning through ancient field systems

What to expect:
Field and coastal paths, some steeper sections

Distance/Time: 7 kilometres/ 4½ miles. Allow 3½ to 4 hours

Start: Bosigran National Trust car park

Grid ref: SW 428 371

Ordnance Survey map: Explorer 104 Redruth & St Agnes

Refreshment: Gurnard's Head, Treen | 01736 796928 | www.gurnardshead.co.uk

Walk outline

From Carn Galver Mine, it's across fields down to the coast before climbing up to Bosigran Castle. The way undulates on across sloping, heath-covered coastal cliffs, winding behind Porthmeor Cove and round to Gurnard's Head. After striking inland to Treen, where there's a pub, it's then a short stretch along a lane before taking to the fields once more past Lower Porthmeor and Bosigran Farm back to the start.

Carn Galver

The two ruined buildings beside the road were engine houses for the Carn Galver tin mine; that to the west driving a pump lifting water from the workings, while the other winched up the ore. The mine shaft was 130 fathoms deep, although an adit at 70 fathoms ran out to the head of the beach at Porthmoina Cove. The mine was intermittently worked for over 30 years, employing upwards of 70 men at its peak. But, despite the installation of a steam engine to pump out water, it was plagued by flooding and never very profitable, producing only 150 tons of tin before it finally closed in 1878.

Carn Galver dawn

Common blue butterfly

The Walk

1. Head from the road towards the coast on a path leaving to the left of the **Carn Galver engine house chimney**. Through a gate, stick with the main path to go through another gate, and keep going. Just beyond a third gate, near **ruins** above **Porthmoina Cove**, branch right to join the crossing **Coast Path**.

2. Climb steeply to **Bosigran Castle**, *the site of an Iron Age settlement*. At the highpoint the path swings right, picking up a boundary wall to reach a granite **Coast Path marker**. Over a stile on the left, the way runs clear across the bracken hillside to the head of **Halldrine Cove**. After another stiff pull, the way undulates more easily above the head of the narrow inlet of **Great Zawn** before gaining height again onto the next **headland**. Beyond, the path gently falls, crossing a stile above **Porthmeor Cove**.

3. Stick with the **Coast Path** over a sturdy granite bridge, climbing beyond onto **Porthmeor Cliff**. The path winds on more easily above the cliffs. Eventually descend from **Treen Cliff** to meet a crossing path.

4. The path left drops onto **Gurnard's Head**, but the way back rises to the right. Shortly joined by another path, keep

going towards cottages at **Treen**. Over a stile, continue beside the edge of a couple of fields and then up **steps** into another field. Carry on to leave through a small gate (not the field gate), crossing a final stile onto a street. Walk past houses to a junction by the **Gurnard's Head Inn**.

5. Follow the road right for 800 metres to **Porthmeor**. Approaching the village, watch for a field gate on the right just before a telegraph pole. Leave immediately after the gate over a stile into the adjacent field and head out past a **standing stone** to a stile at the far side. Past **barns**, keep going in the same direction over more stiles, passing between **cottages** and then dropping over

© Crown copyright and/or database right. All rights reserved. Licence number 100047867

Semi-wild pony on the cliffs above Gurnard's Head

a **bridge**. Climb away onto a rising path leading to **Bosigran Farm**.

6. Crossing a stile into the yard, walk toward the **main house** before turning right on a path beside **barns**. Through gates, go forward on a track with a wall on your right. Keep ahead beyond its corner, passing through another gate in front to put a wall now on your left.

In the next field, swing left with the wall and carry on at the edge of two more fields. Then veer right to a gate part way along the far boundary and walk across yet another field. Through a gap, bear left to meet your outward route.

Follow it up through a gate and back to **Bosigran car park** to complete the walk. ◆

Local delicacy?

Pilchards were once landed and processed in Treen Cove, but the adjacent headland is named for its resemblance to the gurnard, a bottom dwelling prehistoric-looking fish with long, spiny fins. Having an earthy flavour it was never regarded as a delicacy, but sometimes added to stock or fish stew. More often it was used simply as bait for lobster pots, that is, until rebranded by celebrity chefs. So maybe you should give it a try after all.

Poldark Country's iconic Crowns mines at Botallack

Cape Cornwall

A long but spectacular ramble past Cornwall's most impressive coastal mining remains

What to expect:
Good coastal and inland paths and tracks, but some steeper ascents

Distance/Time: 11 kilometres/ 7 miles. Allow 3¼ to 4 hours

Start: Cape Cornwall National Trust car park (pay and display)

Grid ref: SW 353 317

Ordnance Survey map: Explorer 102 Land's End

Refreshment: NT Count House Workshop, Botallack | 01736 786004 | www.nationaltrust.org.uk/botallack; OR The Queens Arms, Botallack | 01736 788318 | queensarms-botallack.co.uk

Walk Outline

Start by walking past St Helen's Chapel onto Cape Cornwall, before returning inland via Boswedden to the Kenidjack valley. Skirt Botallack village to pass the extensive remains of its mining ventures, then follow a track to the Levant Mine, along the coast. The way back explores more ruins above Botallack Head before rejoining the Coast Path. After a detour to the dramatic Crown mines engine houses, continue to the Kenidjack valley, there detouring again to more ruins at Porth Ledden. The final leg follow the cliffs back to Cape Cornwall.

Cornish mining

Rich lodes of Cornish tin, copper and other metal ores have been exploited since the Bronze Age. Cornish tin was traded across the known world, initially panned from alluvial deposits but later dug from mines. During the 18th century, steam power pumped water, raised men and ore to the surface and processed it for smelting, enabling ever deeper mines, some extending far beneath the sea. For a hundred years, Cornish tin and copper supplied much of the world's needs and vast sums were made by mine owners and entrepreneurs. The last Cornish mine, South Crofty closed in 1998.

Wheal Owles Engine House

Peregrine and prey

The Walk

1. First of all, walk up onto **Cape Cornwall** for the views, barely 800 metres less westerly than Land's End. Out of the **car park**, cross to a gate opposite and follow a path half-left past the ruin of **St Helen's Chapel**. Through a gate climb onto the **headland**, the high point marked by a towering **chimney cum navigation aid**. Return to the car park and walk up the lane, following it around a sharp right bend at the top of the hill.

2. At the next bend, turn off left and walk to the end of the street. Go right and the through a gate to follow a field edge path. Passing a stile partway along the second field, strike left across to another stile and continue the line across successive fields towards houses at **Boscean**, eventually following a wall on the right into the corner. Over a stile, turn left to find **steps** onto the top of a broad wall, which leads out to a track.

The distinctive tall buildings and associated chimneys dotting the Cornish landscape were built to house massive beam engines, used to pump water from the mines. Installed around 1715, the first practical engines were 'atmospheric engines' designed by Newcomen, but

these used phenomenal quantities of coal, which had to be transported at great cost from Wales. James Watt's improvements, principally introducing a separate condensation chamber in 1776, brought a four-fold increase in efficiency and further dramatic advances came with Trevithick's developments at the beginning of the 19th century which, for the

© Crown copyright and/or database right. All rights reserved. Licence number 100047867

The Levant Mine features a restored steam-powered beam engine

first time employed the use of high pressure steam. Such engines remained largely the mainstay of power throughout the mining era, being also used to drive whinns (winding machines to haul ore to the surface) and stamping machines, which pounded the ore into small pieces before being roasted and smelted to release the metal within.

3. Go left past **farm buildings**. Where the track then forks, bear right on a footpath that winds left of a **chimney** into the valley below. Over a **bridge**, cross a track diagonally right to a path and climb

away. Bend right and left to meet another track at **Kenidjack Farm**. Keep ahead across overgrown heath, climbing a stile and passing a **disused mine** to come out by houses. Go right and immediately left on a rough track. Where that later bends right, bear left with a bridleway. But as that then swings right, keep ahead over a stile, and walk out between **cottages** to another track. Veer right to emerge onto a lane at **Botallack**.

4. Turn left and keep left at a junction, curving left again past a second junction on a track leading to the National Trust's

The Crowns engine houses cling to the cliffs on Cornwall's 'Tin Coast'

Botallack Mine car park. Carry on along the track past the extensive ruins of the mine for another 1.5 kilometres to a second **car park** at **Levant Mine**. Again the remains are spread over a wide area, the main centre being down to the left beyond the car park.

5. To return, go back the way you came past the car park, to find the **Coast Path** forking off right after some 800 metres. Further on, it briefly rejoins the track, before branching off again below the **arsenic works at Botallack**. Just beyond, by a **chimney** a path drops back right across the cliffs to the two engine houses at **Crowns**.

6. Climb back to regain the coast path and follow it on, before long passing **Wheale Owles**. Keep ahead as another path joins, branching off right with the **Coast Path** a little further along to ruins above **Zawn Buzz** and **Zawn Gen**.

7. Dropping to a track (which leads right to an **impressive view point**) turn left. Shortly, fork off right with the **Coast Path** and drop to a track along the base of the **Kenidjack valley**. To the right a detour leads to more **ruins** above **Porth Ledden**.

8. Head back up the valley. Just past a cottage, the **Coast Path** is signed off

...ht, crossing a **stream** and winding ... the opposite side to meet a crossing ...th.

...Go right towards Cape Cornwall, ...ortly joining a track. Keep right again

to come out on the lane above the **Cape Cornwall car park**. A parallel field path avoids a last stretch on tarmac, completing the walk. ♦

The Botallack arsenic labyrinth

By the 19th century, arsenic appeared in anything from medicines to dyes and wood preserver to rat killer, not to mention a means of dispatching your spouse. Present as an impurity in tin, it was removed by roasting the ore and condensed from the gases in a maze of tunnels as a white powder. When all had cooled, children were sent in to scrape it from the walls, protected only by a handkerchief across their mouth and a smear of mud over exposed skin.

Useful Information

Visit North Cornwall
South Cornwall's official tourism website covers everything from accommodation and events to attractions and adventure: **www.visitcornwall.com/places/north-cornwall**

Cornwall AONB
www.cornwall-aonb.gov.uk

Selected Tourist Information Centres
The main TICs provide free information on everything from accommodation and transport to what's on and walking advice.

Boscastle	01840 250010
Bude	01288 354240
Newquay	01637 828516
Padstow	01841 533449
Perranporth	01872 575254
Redruth	01209 216760
St Ives	01736 788165
St Just	01736 788165
Sennen Cove	01736 871215
Tintagel	01840 779084

Rail Travel
Main stations are located in Truro and Penzance with others serving the coast at Newquay, Hayle and St Ives.

National Rail Enquiries 08457 484950 or **www.nationalrail.com.uk**

Bus Travel
Many places along the North Cornwall Coast are served by bus: **www.travelinesw.c**

Camping
Cornwall is a popular area for camping, with many sites owned by or affiliated to the Camp and Caravanning Club: 024 7647 5426 | **www.campingandcaravanningclub.co.uk**